THE CONCISE
DICTIONARY OF
SCOTTISH QUOTATIONS

Crombie Jardine
Publishing Limited
Unit 17,
196, Rose Street,
Edinburgh,
EH2 4AT
www.crombiejardine.com

This edition was first published by
Crombie Jardine Publishing Limited in 2006

ISBN 10: 1-905102-89-5
ISBN 13: 978-1-905102-89-1

Written by Betty Kirkpatrick

Typeset by Ben Ottridge

Printed and bound in Great Britain by
William Clowes Ltd, Beccles, Suffolk

Dedication

For my grandchildren
Iain, Conall, Flora, Corin and Rory.

INTRODUCTION

In the second part of the twentieth century there began to be a marked increase in the number of reference books available in bookshops. No longer was the reference library of the average fairly educated household restricted to one dictionary, probably dog-eared and several decades old, one out-dated copy of Roget's Thesaurus, either much-thumbed or pristine, according to the needs of the household, and possibly an old copy of Fowler's English Usage.

This increased interest in reference publishing started with dictionaries and a great variety of these, in various shapes and sizes, began to be made available to the public. This sparked off an interest in other kinds of reference books. Existing ones began to be regularly updated and a whole deluge of new ones appeared. These included thesauruses, guides to good usage, guides to good grammar, guides to correct spelling, hints on how to improve your writing, books of idioms and so on.

They also included a varied range of books of quotations. A quotation in the context of dictionaries of quotations is a piece of writing by someone, usually someone well-known, that seems so apt or memorable that other people refer to it in their own speech or writing. Up till that point, there had really been only one well-known dictionary of quotations and this was the Oxford Dictionary of Quotations. Now many more became available and seemed to whet the public's appetite.

Some people use dictionaries of quotations like this one simply for the pleasure of browsing through them. Browsing, after all, is one of the invaluable uses of reference books and a great deal of knowledge can be acquired in a relatively painless way when browsing.

Browsers of dictionaries of quotations may find pleasure in identifying a quotation that seems particularly appropriate to some situation in their own lives. However, some people may use a dictionary of quotations, such as this one, for a more specific purpose. They may, for example, use a dictionary of quotations to find out the source of something they have encountered in their reading, or to check the exact wording of a quotation they half-remember.

Many people use dictionaries of quotations seeking inspiration for a speech which they have to make. A quotation makes an excellent hook on which to hang an after-dinner speech, as many people have discovered.

This particular dictionary of quotations is, of course, culled mainly from Scottish writers, although some quotations have been included from English writers referring to the Scots or Scotland. We do like to know what other people are saying about us!

The quotations in this book are mainly historical, many of them having their source in well-known older Scottish writers, although other professions are also represented. Scotland is fortunate in having had so many famous writers who wrote so prolifically and so memorably. Indeed, you could easily fill a considerably larger book than this with memorable quotations from Robert Burns alone.

As well as quotations this book contains many traditional sayings and proverbs. There is a wealth of these, from weather hints to advice on diet and health and how to look after your money. Several of them are as true as they are succinct.

A short glossary has been added as a guide to the Scots words in the book. This is particularly useful with reference to the traditional sayings and proverbs which contain many Scots words. It will be useful, too, for those writers who have penned their thoughts in Scots, although many of the famous quoted writers wrote in English.

Betty Kirkpatrick
2006

William Alexander, Sir
(c.1567-1640), courtier,
poet and politician

The deepest rivers make least din,
The silent soule doth most abound in care

Aurora (1604)

The weaker sex, to piety more prone

Doomsday

What thing so good which not some harme may
bring?
Even to be happy is a dangerous thing

Darius (1603)

Isabel Alison (d.1681),
Covenanter

I leave my testimony against all the blood shed
on both scaffolds, and in the fields, and seas; and
against all the cruelty used against the people of
the Lord—I leave my testimony against profanity
of all sorts, and likewise against lukewarmness
and indifference in the Lord's matter

*The Dying Testimony and Last Words of Isabel Alison
(January, 1681)*
She was hanged in Edinburgh for publicly protesting against
the cruel treatment of those who were Sympathizers of
the Covenanters

John Arbuthnot (1667-1735),
physician and humorist

Law is a bottomless pit

The name of a satirical pamphlet (1712)

Hame's hame, be it ever so hamely

The History of John Bull (1712)

All political parties die at last of swallowing their
own lies

Robert Ayton, Sir (1570-1638), poet and courtier

To live upon Tabacco and on hope,
The ones but smoake, the other is but winde

Upone Tabacco

Yes, I have died for love, as others do;
But praised by God, it was in such a sort
That I revived within an hour or two

On Love

William Edmonstoune Aytoun (1813-65), lawyer and humorist

There was glory on his forehead,
There was lustre in his eye,
And he never walked to battle,
More proudly than to die

The Execution of Montrose, Lays of the Scottish Cavaliers (1849)

Nowhere beats the hearts so kindly
As beneath the tartan plaid

Lays of the Scottish Cavaliers (1849)

Joanna Baillie (1762-1851), playwright and poet

But poverty parts good company

Poverty Parts Good Company

Ladies of four score and upwards cannot expect
to be robust, and need not be gay

From a letter to Mary Somerville (1843)

The theatre is a school in which much good or
evil may be learned

A Series of Plays (1798)

Alexander Bain (1818-1903), Scottish philosopher and psychologist

Instinct is untaught ability

Senses and Intellect

Arthur James Balfour (1848-1930), Conservative politician and British Prime Minister

History does not repeat itself. Historians repeat each other

The energies of our system will decay; the glory of the sun will be dimmed, and the earth, tideless and inert, will no longer tolerate the race which has for a moment disturbed its solitude. Man will go down into the pit and all his thoughts will perish

The Foundation of Belief (1895)

It is unfortunate, considering that enthusiasm moves the world, that so few enthusiasts can be trusted to speak the truth

From a letter to Mrs Drew (1918)

Lady Frances Balfour (1858-1931), writer and suffragist

Golf has ceased to be a peculiarly national game. It is now no longer a pastime for the impecunious Scot, armed with two or three clubs, and a feather ball, it has become a professional sport, pursued by devastating hordes of foreigners among whom the American tongue rises shrill and strident

Ne Obliviscaris: Dinna Forget (1930)

Arthur Balmerino, Lord (1688-1746), Jacobite

I shall die with a true heart and undaunted; for I think no man fit to live that is not fit to die; nor am I in any ways concerned at what I have done

Said to one of his prison visitors before his execution in London in August 1746

J M Barrie, Sir (1860-1937), playwright and novelist

We are undoubtedly a sentimental people, and it sometimes plays havoc with that other celebrated sense of ours, the practical

From a speech to the Royal Scottish Corporation on 30 November 1928

The scientific man is the only person who has anything new to say and who does not know how to say it

James Beattie (1735-1803), philosopher and poet

We who live in Scotland are obliged to study English from books, like a dead language which we can understand but cannot speak. Our style smells of the lamp and we are slaves of the language, and are continually afraid of committing gross blunders

Quoted in An Account of the Life and Writings of James Beattie LL D (1806)

John Hamilton Belhaven, Lord
(1656-1708)

None can destroy Scotland, save Scotland's self;
hold your hands from the pen, you are secure

From a speech beseeching the Scottish parliament (November 1706) not to sign the Treaty of Union with England, quoted in Daniel Defoe's History of the Union (1785)

Isabella Bird (1831-1904),
English traveller and writer

There were dirty little children as usual rolling
in the gutter or sitting stolidly on the kerb-stone;
as usual, haggard, wrinkled, vicious faces were
looking out of the dusty windows above, and an
air of joylessness, weariness, and struggle hung
over all

Notes on Old Edinburgh (1869)

Limited water and unlimited whisky, crowded
dens and unwholesome air; we need nothing
more to make a city full of drunkards

Notes on Old Edinburgh (1869)

John Stuart Blackie (1809-95), linguist and nationalist

Who owns these ample hills?—a lord who lives
ten months in London and in Scotland two;
O'er the wide moors with gun in hand he drives;
And, Scotland, this is all he knows of you!

*Absentee Proprietor, Lays and Legends of Ancient Greece
and other poems (1857)*

James Boswell (1740-95), biographer of Samuel Johnson

Dr Johnson expatiated rather too strongly upon
the benefits derived to Scotland from the Union,
and the bad state of the people before it. I am
entertained with his copious exaggeration upon
that subject: but I am uneasy when people are by,
who do not know him as well as I do, and may be
apt to think him narrow-minded. I therefore
diverted the subject

Journal of a Tour of the Hebrides (1786)

For my own part, I think no innocent species of wit or pleasantry should be suppressed; and that a good pun may be admitted among the smaller excellencies of lively conversation

Life of Samuel Johnson (1791)

We cannot tell the precise moment when friendship is formed. As in filling a vessel drop by drop, there is at last a drop that makes it run over; so in a series of kindnesses, there is at last one which makes the heart run over

Life of Samuel Johnson (1791)

Braham Seer (c.16th/17th century), Highland prophet

Oh! Drummossie, thy bleak moor shall, ere many generations have passed away, be stained with the best blood of the Highlands. Glad am I that I will not see that day, for it will be a fearful period; heads will be lopped off by the score, and no mercy will be shown or quarter given on either side

The Prophecies of the Braham Seer by Alexander Mackenzie (1977); the prophecy here is said to foretell the bloody battle of Culloden

Sheep shall eat men, men will eat sheep, the black rain will eat all things; in the end old men shall return from new lands

The Prophecies of the Braham Seer by Alexander Mackenzie (1977); the prophecy is said to foretell the clearances and depopulation of the Highlands and their later repopulation

William Brodie (Deacon Brodie) (1741-88), respectable cabinet-maker by day, burglar by night

And lastly my neck being now about to be embraced by a halter I recommend to all rogues, sharpers, thieves and gamblers, as well in high as in low stations, to take care of theirs by leaving all wicked practices and becoming good members of society

From his last will and testament composed on the day he was executed (October, 1788)

John Buchan (1875-1940), novelist

The dominant thought of youth is the bigness of the world, of age its smallness. As we grow older we escape from the tyranny of matter and recognize that the true centre of gravity is the mind

Memory Hold-the-Door (1940)

Henry Thomas Buckle (1821-62), English historian

Even in the capital of Scotland, in that centre of intelligence, which once boasted of being the modern Athens, a whisper will circulate that such a one is to be avoided, for that he is a free-thinker, as if free-thinking were a crime, or as if it were not better to be a free-thinker than a slavish thinker

History of Civilization (1857-62)

Robert Burns (1759-96), poet and song-writer

But Mousie, thou art no thy lane,
In proving foresight may be vain:
The best-laid schemes o' mice and men
Gang aft agley,
An' leave us nought but grief an' pain,
For promis'd joy!

To a Mouse (1785)
Much quoted lines commenting on the essential fallibility of plans and hopes. The shortened quote 'the best laid schemes' has become a cliché in English

Princes and lords are but the breath of kings,
'An honest man's the noblest work o' God'

*The Cottar's Saturday Night (1785), Burns here quoting
Alexander Pope*

Then gently scan your brother Man,
Still gentler sister woman,
Tho' they may gang a kennin' wrang,
To step aside is human

Address to the Unco' Guid (1786)
Lines urging people to refrain from passing judgment on others

O wad some Power the giftie gie us
To see oursels as ithers see us!
It wad frae monie a blunder free us,
An' foolish notion

To a Louse (1786)
Poem written when Burns saw such a creature on a lady's hat in church, lines indicating that we would not behave so foolishly if we could view ourselves with the eyes of others

But facts are chiels that winna ding
An downa be disputed

  A Dream (1786)

Man's inhumanity to Man
Makes countless thousands mourn

  Man was Made to Mourn—A Dirge (1786)

Fair fa' your honest, sonsie face,
Great chieftain o' the puddin' race!
Aboon them a' ye tak your place,
Painch, tripe, or thairm,
Weel are ye wordy o' a grace
As lang's my airm

  To a Haggis (1786)

I myself can affirm, from both bachelor and
wedlock experience, that love is the Alpha and
Omega of human enjoyment

  Letter to Alexander Cunningham (1789)

John Anderson, my jo, John,
When we were first acquent;
Your locks were like the raven,
Your bonie brow was brent;
But now your brow is beld, John,
Your locks are like the snaw,
But blessings on your frosty pow,
John Anderson, my jo!

A poem about older love (1790)

My heart's in the Highlands, my heart is not here,
My heart's in the Highlands a-chasing the deer,
A-chasing the wild deer and following the roe.
My heart's in the highlands, wherever I go

(1790)

Ah! gentle dames, it gars me greet
To think how mony counsels sweet,
How mony lengthen'd, sage advices,
The husband frae the wife despises!

Tam o' Shanter (1790)

But pleasures are like poppies spread,
You seize the flower, its bloom is shed,
Or like the snow falls in the river,
A moment white—then melts forever;
Or like the borealis race,
That flit ere you can point their place:
Or like the rainbow's lovely form
Evanishing amid the storm,
Nae man can tether time or tide;
The hour approaches Tam maun ride

Tam o' Shanter (1790)
The lines demonstrate that Burns could be lyrical in English
as well Scots

Inspiring bold John Barleycorn!
What dangers thou canst make us scorn!
Wi tippeny, we fear nae evil;
Wi usquabae, we'll face the devil!

Tam o' Shanter (1790)
Tippeny is ale and usquabae is whisky and so Burns is here
stressing the power of the so-called Dutch courage

Ae fond kiss, and then we sever!
Ae fareweel, and then for ever!
Deep in heart-wrung tears I'll pledge thee,
Warring sighs and groans I'll wage thee

Ae Fond Kiss (1791)
Lines from one of the most moving poems of lost love

Had we never lov'd sae kindly,
Had we never lov'd sae blindly,
Never met—or never parted
We had ne'er been broken-hearted

Ae Fond Kiss (1791)

Ye banks and braes o' bonie Doon,
How can ye bloom sae fresh and fair;
How can ye chant ye little birds,
And I sae weary fu' o' care!
Thou'll break my heart thou warbling bird,
That wantons thro' the flowering thorn:
Thou mindst me o' departed joys,
Departed, never to return

The Banks o' Doon (1791)

Here's freedom to him that wad read,
Here's freedom to him that wad write!
There's nane ever feared that the truth should
be heard,
But they wham the truth would indite

Here's a Health to them that's Awa' (1792)

Fareweel to o' our Scottish fame,
Fareweel our ancient glory;
Sae fam'd in martial story!
Now Sark rins o'er the Solway sands,
And Tweed rins to the ocean,
To mark where England's province stands,
Such a parcel of rogues in a nation!

Such a Parcel of Rogues in a Nation (1792)

But pith and power, till my last hour,
I'll mak this declaration:
We're bought and sold for English gold,
Such a parcel of rogues in a nation!

Such a Parcel of Rogues in a Nation (1792)

O my love's like a red, red rose
That's newly sprung in June;
O my love's like a melodie
That's sweetly play'd in tune
As fair art thou, my bonie lass,
So deep in love am I;
And I will love thee still, my dear,
Till a' the seas gang dry

(1794)
One of the world's most famous love songs

Then let us pray that come it may,
As come it will, for a' that,
That sense and worth, o'er a' the earth'
Shall bear the gree, an a' that;
For a' that and a' that,
It's comin' yet for a' that,
That man to man the world o'er,
Shall brothers be for a' that.

For a' that and a' that (1795)
A poem that has gained international renown as a kind of
hymn to equality. It was sung at the opening of the Scottish
Parliament

A child's amang you takin notes,
And, faith, he'll prent it

> *On the Late Captain Grose's Peregrinations thro' Scotland*
> *(1793)*
> **Often used as a warning to someone to be careful what**
> **they say in front of a person who is present**

Lord Byron (1788-1824),
poet

England! thy beauties are tame and domestic,
To one who has rov'd on the mountains afar;
Oh! For the crags that are wild and majestic,
The steep frowning glories of dark Loch na Garr

> *Lachin Y Gair, Hours of Idleness (1806)*

Marriage from love, like vinegar from wine—
a sad, sour, sober beverage-by time
Is sharpen'd from its high celestial flavour
Down to a very homely household savour

> *Don Juan (1819-24), Canto 3*

Man's love is of his life a thing apart,
'Tis woman's whole existence

Don Juan (1819-24), Canto 1

But I am half a Scot by birth, and bred
A whole one

Don Juan (1819-24), Canto 10

I scotched, not killed the Scotchman in my blood,
And love the land of mountain and of flood

Don Juan (1819-24), Canto 10

'Tis strange-but true; for Truth is always
Stranger than fiction

Don Juan (1819-24), Canto 14

Donald Cameron, Cameron of Lochiel (c.1695-1748), chief of Clan Cameron

I will share the fate of my prince, and so shall every man over whom nature or fortune hath given me any power

Said to Prince Charles Edward Stewart (August, 1745)

Colin Campbell, Sir (Lord Clyde) (1796-1863), soldier

Bring forward the tartan! Let my own lads at them!

Said when ordering the 93rd Highlanders to launch an attack at the Relief of Lucknow (1857)

Thomas Campbell (1777-1844), poet

And call they this improvement?—to have changed
My native Clyde, thy once romantic shore,
Where nature's face is banished and estranged,
And Heaven reflected in thy wave no more;
Whose banks, that sweetened Mayday's breath before,
Lie sere and leafless now in summer's beam,
With sooty exhalations covered o'er;
And for the daisied green sward, down thy stream
Unsightly brick-lanes smoke, and clanking engines gleam

Lines on Revisiting a Scottish River (1827)

'Tis distance lends enchantment to the view,
And robes the mountain in its azure hue

Pleasures of Hope (1799)

Henry Campbell-Bannerman (1836-1908), Liberal Scottish MP and British Prime Minister

When is a war not a war? When it is carried on by methods of barbarism in South Africa

From a speech given in protest against the British brutal treatment of the Boers (1901)

I seldom venture as you have done into the wilds of the Scotch Highlands. They are not the working and really dominant part of the country: I find the humdrum Lowlands interesting enough: and I keep my temper even by avoiding even the sight of the shooting tenant and ghilliedom which is the curse of Celtic Caledonia

Letter (1905) quoted in A Life of Sir Henry Campbell-Bannerman (1973)

Good government can never be a substitute for government by the people themselves

Speech at Stirling (1905)

Personally I am a great believer in bed, in constantly keeping horizontal

Letter to Mrs Whiteley

Alexander (known as Jupiter) Carlyle (1722-1805), minister and scholar

Since we began to affect speaking a foreign language, which the English dialect is to us, humour, it must be confessed, is less apparent in conversation

Autobiography (1860)

Liquor, without which no Scotch gentleman in those day could be exhilarated

Autobiography (1860)
The liquor referred to was claret

Jane Welsh Carlyle (1801-66), letter writer and diarist, wife of Thomas Carlyle

If I have an antipathy for any class of people it is for fine ladies

Letter to Eliza Miles (1832)

On the whole, tho' English ladies seem to have their wits more at their finger-ends and have a great advantage over me in that respect, I never cease to be glad that I was born on the other side of the Tweed and that those who are nearest and dearest to me are Scotch

Letter to her mother-in-law (1834)

I am more and more persuaded that there is no complete misery in the world that does not emanate from the bowels

Letter to Eliza Stoddart (1834)

Let no woman who values peace of soul ever dream of marrying an author

Letter to John Sterling (1837)

My dear, if Mr Carlyle's digestion had been better there is no telling what he might have done

Remark made to Mrs Oliphant and quoted by the latter in an article on Thomas Carlyle published in Macmillan's Magazine (1881)

When one has been threatened with a great injustice, one accepts a smaller as a favour

Diary entry (November, 1855)

Thomas Carlyle (1795-1881), historian and essayist

Men are grown mechanical in head and heart, as well in hand

Signs of the Times (1829) Critical and Miscellaneous Essays

A man willing to work, and unable to find work, is perhaps the saddest sight that fortune's inequality exhibits under this sun

Chartism (1839)

A well-written Life is almost as rare as a well-spent one

Jean Paul Friedrich Richter (1827), Critical and Miscellaneous Essays

No Scotchman of his time was more entirely Scotch than Walter Scott: the good and the not so good, which all Scotchmen inherit, ran through every fibre of him

Sir Walter Scott (1838), Critical and Miscellaneous Essays

Silence is deep as Eternity; speech is shallow as Time

Sir Walter Scott (1838), Critical and Miscellaneous Essays

In the long run every Government is the exact symbol of its People, with their wisdom and their unwisdom; we have to say, Like People like Government

Past and Present (1843)

Talk that does not end in any kind of action is better suppressed altogether

Inaugural address when Rector of Edinburgh University (1866)

If Jesus Christ were to come today, people would not even crucify him. They would ask him to dinner, and hear what he had to say, and make fun of it

Carlyle at His Zenith (1927) by D A Wilson.

Andrew Carnegie (1835-1919), industrialist and philanthropist

What Benares is to the Hindoo, Mecca to the Mohammedan, Jerusalem to the Christian, all this is Dunfermline to me

Our Coaching Trip (1882)

There is an unwritten law among the best workmen: 'Thou shalt not take thy neighbour's job'

Forum (August, 1886)

Surplus wealth is a sacred trust which its possessor is bound to administer in his lifetime for the good of the community

Wealth, North American Review (1889)

Golf is an indispensable adjunct to high civilization

Said when leaving a large sum of money to Yale University to build a golf course

King Charles I (1600-49)

I die a Christian, according to the profession of the Church of England, as I found it left to me by my father

Said on the scaffold just before he was executed (January, 1649)

John Cleveland (1613-58), English satirical poet

Like Jews they spread, and as Infection flie,
As if the Divell had Ubiquitie.
Hence 'tis they live as Rovers; and defie
This or that Place, Rags of Geographie.
They're Citizens o' the World; they're all in all,
Scotland's a Nation Epidemicall

The Rebel Scot (1644)
The lines refer particularly to Scots who travelled to England
to take part in the English Civil War

Alison Cockburn, Mrs (1712-94), poet and song-writer

I am just returned from a Highland expedition and was much delighted with the magnificence of nature in her awful simplicity

From a letter to David Hume

Henry Cockburn, Lord (1779-1854), judge

Dinner is the English meal, breakfast the Scotch. An Englishman's certainty of getting a good dinner seems to make him indifferent about his breakfast, while the substantiality of a Scotchman's breakfast impairs, or at least might impair, his interest in his dinner

Circuit Journeys (1841)

I never see a scene of Scotch beauty, without being thankful that I have beheld it before it has been breathed over by the angel of mechanical destruction.

Circuit Journeys (1846)

No apology is thought necessary for murdering a tree; many for preserving it

Memorials of his Time (1856)

T W H Crosland,
English poet and journalist

After illicit love and flaring drunkenness, nothing appeals so much to Scotch sentiment as having been born in the gutter

The Unspeakable Scot (1902), The Bard

Under the inspiring tutelage of the National Bard, Scotland has become one of the drunkenest nations in the world

The Unspeakable Scot (1902), The Scot in his Cups

Declaration of Arbroath, The

But, after all, if this prince (Robert Bruce) shall leave the principles he hath so nobly pursued, and consent that we or our kingdom be subjected to the king or to the people of England, we will immediately endeavour to expel him, as our enemy, and as the subverter both of his own and our rights, and will make another king, who will defend our liberties; for, so long as there shall but one hundred of us remain alive, we will never subject ourselves to the domination of the English. For it is not glory, it is not riches, neither is it honour, but it is freedom alone that we fight and contend for, which no honest man will lose but with his life

Signed in 1320, the Declaration was sent to Pope John XXII and sought to ensure recognition of Scotland's independence from England

Arthur Conan Doyle, Sir (1859-1930), novelist, creator of Sherlock Holmes

London, that great cesspool into which all the loungers of the Empire are irresistibly drained

A Study in Scarlet (1887)

How often have I said to you that when you have eliminated the impossible, whatever remains, *however improbable,* must be the truth!

The Sign of Four (1890)

It is a capital mistake to theorize before one has data. Insensibly one begins to twist facts to suit theories, instead of theories to suit facts

A Scandal in Bohemia, Adventures of Sherlock Holmes (1891)

It is my belief, Watson, founded upon my experience, that the lowest and vilest alleys in London do not present a more dreadful record of sin than the smiling and beautiful countryside

The Adventure of the Copper Beeches, Adventures of Sherlock Holmes (1891)

Henry Dundas (1st Viscount Melville) (1742-1811), statesman and lawyer, Lord Advocate

When it is said that no alternative is left to the New Englanders but to starve or rebel, this is not the fact, for there is another way, to submit

Said in a speech to the House of Commons (1775)
Showing clearly his fierce opposition to the American colonists and his determination not to allow them any concessions

Adam Ferguson (1723-1816), philosopher

Affection operates with the greatest force, where it meets with the greatest difficulties: In the breast of the parent, it is most solicitous amidst the dangers and distresses of the child: In the breast of a man, its flame redoubles where the wrongs or sufferings of his friend, or his country, require his aid

An Essay on the History of Civil Society (1767)

Robert Fergusson
(1750-74), poet

Fergusson is now considered to have been a much under-rated poet and he is now regarded as having influenced the work of Robert Burns greatly. His poem, The Farmer's Ingle (1773) is said to have inspired Burns' writing of The Cottar's Saturday Night

For nought can cheer the heart sae weel
As can a canty Highland reel;
It even vivifies the heel
To skip and dance:
Lifeless is he who canna feel
Its influence

The Daft Days (1772)

On Scotia's plains, in days of yore,
When lads and lasses tartan wore,
Saft Music rang on ilka shore,
In hamely weid;
But harmony is now no more,
And music dead

Elegy on the Death of Scots Music (1772)

May Scotia's simmers ay look gay and green
Her yellow har'sts frae scowry blasts decreed;
May a' her tenants sit fu' snug and bien,
Frae the hard grip of ails and poortrith freed,
And a lang lasting train o' peaceful hours succeed

The Farmer's Ingle (1773)

Thanks to the gods who made me poor!
No lukewarm friends molest my door,
Who always shew a busy care
For being legatee or heir:
Of this stamp none will ever follow
The youth that's favour'd by Apollo

Rob Fergusson's Last Will (1773)

Susan Edmondstone Ferrier
(1782-1854), novelist

Worldly prudence is very suitable at seventy, but at
seventy it is absolutely disgusting: in the one it is the
result of experience, in the other it is the offspring of
a little mind and a base contracted heart

Letter to Walter Ferrier (1809/10)

It was the saying, sir, of one of the wisest judges who ever sat upon the Scottish bench, that a *poor* clergy is a *pure* clergy; a maxim which deserves to be engraven in letters of gold in every manse in Scotland

Destiny (1831)

Alexander Fleming, Sir (1881-1955), chemist, discoverer of penicillin

This thirst for immediate results is by no means uncommon, but it is extremely harmful. Really valuable research is a long-term affair

The Life of Sir Alexander Fleming (1959) by André Maurois

A good gulp of whisky at bedtime—it's not very scientific, but it helps

A remedy for the common cold ascribed to him

Andrew Fletcher (of Saltoun) (1655-1716), patriot and a fierce opponent of the 1707 Treaty of Union with England

The Scots deserve no pity, if they voluntarily surrender their united and separate interests to the Mercy of an united Parliament, where the English have so vast a Majority

State of the Controversy betwixt United and Separate Parliaments (1706)

Lord have mercy on my poor country that is so barbarously oppressed

Said to have been his dying words (September, 1716)

John Galt (1779-1839), novelist

From the time of the North Briton of the unprincipled Wilkes, a notion has been entertained that the moral spine in Scotland is more flexible than in England. The truth, however, is that an elementary difference exists in the public feelings of the two nations quite as great as in the idioms of their respective dialects. The English are a justice-loving people, according to charter and statute: the Scotch are a wrong-resenting race, according to right and feeling: and the character of liberty among them takes its aspect from that peculiarity

Ringan Gilhaize (1823)

Patrick Geddes, Sir (1854-1932), planner and biologist

When an idea is dead it is embalmed in a textbook

The Worlds of Patrick Geddes (1978) by Philip Boardman

Lewis Grassic Gibbon (pseudonym of James Leslie Mitchell) (1901-35), novelist and journalist

You saw their faces in firelight, father's and mother's, and the neighbours' before the lamps lit up, tired and kind, faces dear and close to you, you wanted the words they'd known and used, forgotten in the far-off youngness of their lives, Scots words to tell to your heart, how they wrung it and held it, the toil of their days and unendingly their fight. And the next minute that passed from you, you were English, back to the English words so sharp and clean and true-for a while, for a while, till they slid so smooth from your throat you knew they could never say anything that was worth the saying at all

Sunset Song (1902) Part 1 Ploughing

The Episcopalian Church in Scotland gave to life and ritual mildly colourful trappings, a sober display; it avoided God with a shudder of genteel distaste

Religion, Scottish Scene (1934)

Jane, Duchess of Gordon (known as Jenny of Monreith) (c.1749-1812), society hostess and a supporter of William Pitt, the Younger

I have been acquainted with David Hume and William Pitt, and therefore I am not afraid to converse with anybody

The quotation appears in A Group of Scottish Women by Harry Graham (1908)

John Graham (of Claverhouse) (Viscount Dundee) (1648-89), Jacobite soldier and an opponent of the Covenanters

To man I can be answerable, and, as for God, I will take Him in my own hands

Said to the widow of a Covenanter whom he had just had shot in front of her

Anne Grant (of Laggan), Mrs (1755-1838), poet and essayist

Enthusiasm is the wine of life; it cheers and supports the mind, though excess, in either case, produces intoxication and madness

Letter to Mrs Brown (February, 1789), Letters from the Mountains (1803)

Fashion is an epidemical frenzy, that follows and overtakes us everywhere though we, in following it, can overtake it nowhere

Letter to Mrs Smith (March, 1789), Letters from the Mountains (1803)

Elizabeth Grant (of Rothiemurchus) (1797-1885), diarist

Except in a real old-fashioned scotch house, where no dish was attempted that was not national, the various abominations served up in corner dishes under French names were merely libels upon housekeeping

Memoirs of a Highland Lady, Chapter 21 (1898)

If old men marry young women, young widows should be left quite independent as some return for the sacrifice, the full extent of which they are not aware of till too late

Memoirs of a Highland Lady, Chapter 25 (1898)

James Grant (1822-87), soldier, historian and novelist

Unfortunately, the old fallacy with regard to the education of women, viz that the higher instruction was not necessary for them, is not yet exploded, but we are slowly realizing that any knowledge calculated to improve the human mind should be communicated to women, no less than men

A History of the Burgh Schools of Scotland, Volume 1 (1876)

Possibly the character of the girls may, by being taught with boys, suffer to some extent from the rough and boisterous manners of their companions; but, on the other hand, it is certain that the boys will suffer *more* from the absence of the girls than the girls from the presence of the boys

A History of the Burgh Schools of Scotland, Volume 1 (1876)

Douglas Haig (1st Earl of Bemersyde) (1861-1928), Commander-in-chief of the British Army (1915-18)

Every position must be held to the last man: there must be no retirement. With our backs to the wall, and believing in the justice of our cause, each one of us must fight on to the end. The safety of our homes and the freedom of mankind alike depend upon the conduct of each one of us at this critical moment

An order issued on April 12, 1918 to the British troops in the trenches to put up maximum resistance to the German offensive.
When the full horror, and, to a great extent, the pointlessness, of the loss of lives in World War I was realized, Earl Haig got much of the blame for faulty leadership

Hailes, Lord, Sir David Dalrymple (1762-92), judge and historian

When we read of facts or customs dissimilar from what we see every day, we generally pronounce them to be fictitious. This is the brief decision of ignorance

Annals of Scotland (1776)

(James) Keir Hardie (1856-1915), Labour politician

I think it could be shown that the position of women, as of most other things, has always been better, nearer to equality, with man, in Celtic, than in non-Celtic, races

The Citizenship of Women (1906)

I often feel sick at heart with politics and all that pertains thereof

A comment made in 1913 and quoted in Contrast in Philosophies by H Addison (1982)

James Hogg (known as the Ettrick Shepherd) (1770-1835), poet and novelist

Having been bred amongst mountains I am always unhappy when in a flat country

Letter to Walter Scott (July, 1802)

Life is a weary, weary, weary,
Life is a weary coble o' care;
The poets mislead you,
Wha ca' it a meadow,
For life is a puddle o' perfect despair

Life is a Weary Coble o' Care

David Hume (1711-76), philosopher

Poets themselves, tho' liars by profession, always endeavour to give an air of truth to their fictions; and where that is totally neglected, their performance, however, ingenious, will never be able to afford much pleasure

A Treatise of Human Nature (1739), Book 1, Part 3

Generally speaking, the errors in religion are dangerous; those in philosophy only ridiculous

A Treatise of Human Nature (1739), Book 1, Part 4

Human nature is the only science of man; and yet has been hitherto the most neglected

A Treatise of Human Nature (1739), Book 1, Part 4

Reason is, and ought only to be, the slave of passions, and can never pretend to any other office than to serve and obey them

A Treatise of Human Nature (1739), Book 2, Part 3

Nothing endears so much a friend as sorrow for his death

Of Tragedy, Essays Moral, Political and Literary 1 (1742)

The great end of all human industry is the attainment of happiness. For this were arts invented, science cultivated, laws ordained and societies modelled by the most profound wisdom of patriots and legislators

The Stoic, Essays Moral, Political and Literary 1 (1742)

Notwithstanding all the Pains which I have taken in the Study of the English Language, I am still jealous of my Pen. As to my Tongue, you have seen, that I regard it as totally desperate and irreclaimable

Letter to John Wilkes (October, 1754)

It is difficult for a man to speak long of himself without vanity; therefore I will be short

My Own Life (published 1777)

James Hutton (1726-97), scientist and geologist

Time, which measures everything in our idea, and is often deficient in our schemes, is to nature endless and as nothing; it cannot limit that by which it alone has existence

Theory of the Earth, Transactions of the Royal Society of Edinburgh (1788)

Elsie Maud Inglis (1864-1917), surgeon and organizer of the Scottish Women's Hospitals

The traditional male disbelief in our capacity cannot be argued away; it can only be worked away

> *Quoted in Margot Lawrence's Biography of Elsie Inglis, Shadows and Swords (1971), Chapter 4*

The worst of being a doctor is that one's mistakes matter so much

> *Quoted in Margot Lawrence's Biography of Elsie Inglis, Shadows and Swords (1971), Chapter 6*

James V (1512-42), King of Scotland (1513-42)

It cam wi' a lass and it will pass wi' a lass

> *Said to be a deathbed comment on learning that a daughter, Mary, had just been born.*
> The 'it' referred to is the Scottish crown which came to the Stewarts by marriage to a lass, Marjorie, daughter of Robert the Bruce

James VI and I (1566-1625), King of Scotland from 1567 and also King of England from 1603

A custome lothsome to the eye, hatefull to the Nose, harmefull to the braine, dangerous to the Lungs, and in the black stinking fume thereof, neerest resembling the horrible Stigian smoke of the pit that is bottomlesse

A Counterblast to Tobacco (1604)

Here I sit and govern Scotland with my pen. I write and it is done; and by the Clerk of the Council I govern Scotland now, which others could not do by the sword

Speech to the English Parliament (1607)

I will govern according to the common weal, but not according to the common will

Address to the House of Commons (December, 1621)

Francis Jeffrey, Lord Jeffrey (1773-1850), critic and judge

Scotch is not to be considered as a provincial dialect—the vehicle only of rustic vulgarity and rude local humour. It is the language of a whole country-long an independent country and still separate in its laws, character and manners

Review of Cromek's Reliques of Robert Burns in Edinburgh Review 26 (January, 1809)

Samuel Johnson, Dr (1709-1784), English lexicographer and writer

OATS—A grain, which in England is generally given to horses, but in Scotland supports the people

A Dictionary of the English Language (1755)

Norway, too, has noble wild prospects, and Lapland is remarkable for its prodigious noble wild prospects. But, Sir, let me tell you, the noblest prospect which a Scotchman ever sees is the high road that leads him to England

Quoted in Life of Samuel Johnson (1791) by James Boswell

Your country consists of two things, stone and water. There is, indeed, a little earth above the stone in some places, but a very little, and the stone is always appearing. It is like a man in rags; the naked skin is till peeping out

Said to Sir Allan Maclean; quoted in Life of Samuel Johnson (1791) by James Boswell

Much may be made of a Scotchman, if he be caught young

Said of Lord Mansfield who was educated in England; quoted in Life of Samuel Johnson (1791) by James Boswell

A Scotchman must be a very sturdy moralist, who does not love Scotland better than truth: he will always love it better than inquiry: and if falsehood flatters his vanity, will not be very diligent to detect it

A Journey to the Western Islands of Scotland (1775)

Seeing Scotland, Madam, is only seeing a worse England. It is seeing the flower gradually fade away to the naked stalk

Said to Mrs Hester Thrale who had expressed a wish to visit Scotland, quoted in Life of Samuel Johnson (1791) by James Boswell

Henry Home Kames, Lord (1696-1782), judge and philosopher

A man says what he knows: a woman what is agreeable: knowledge is necessary to the former; taste is sufficient to the latter

Loose Hints upon Education, chiefly concerning the Culture of the Heart (1782)

Women, destined by nature to be obedient, ought to be disciplined early to bear wrongs without murmuring

Loose Hints upon Education, chiefly concerning the Culture of the Heart (1782)

A boy who is flogged into grammar rules makes a shift to apply them; but he applies them by rote, like a parrot. Boys, for a knowledge they acquire of any language, are not indebted to dry rules, but to practice and observation

Loose Hints upon Education, chiefly concerning the Culture of the Heart (1782)

Kelvin, Lord (William Thomson) (1824-1907), scientist and inventor

The earth is filled with evidence that it has not been going on for ever in the present state, and that there is a progress of events towards a state infinitely different from the present

From a lecture to the Geological Society of Glasgow (February, 1868)

I often say that when you can measure what you are speaking about, and express it in numbers, you know something about it: but when you cannot express it in numbers, your knowledge is of a meagre and unsatisfactory kind: it may be the beginning of knowledge, but you have scarcely, in your thoughts, advanced to the stage of *science*

From a lecture to the Institution of Civil Engineers (May, 1871)

Paradoxes have no place in science. Their removal is the substitution of true for false statements and thoughts

From an Address to the Royal Institution (1887)

Do not be afraid of being free-thinkers. If you think strongly enough you will be forced by science to the belief in God, which is the foundation of all Religion. You will find science not antagonistic, but helpful, to Religion

From a vote of thanks in response to a course of lectures on Christian Apologetics given by The Reverend Professor Henslow in London (1903)

John Knox (c.1513-72), Protestant church reformer

To promote a Woman to beare rule, superioritie, dominion, or empire above any Realme, Nation or Citie, is repugnant to Nature; contumlie to God, a thing most contrarious to his revealed will and approved ordinance

The First Blast of the Trumpet against the Monstrous Regiment of Women (1558)
This was a work written as a condemnation of female rule such as that of Mary of Guise, Regent of Scotland, Mary Stewart, Mary Queen of Scots and Mary Tudor, Queen of England

Woman in her greatest perfection was made to serve and obey man, not to rule and command him

The First Blast of the Trumpet against the Monstrous Regiment of Women (1558)
see previous quotation

Charles Lamb (1775-1834), English essayist

I have been trying all my life to like Scotchmen, and am obliged to desist from the experiment in despair

Jews, Quakers, Scotchmen, and other Imperfect Sympathies published in London Magazine (August, 1821)

Andrew Lang (1844-1912), poet, essayist and journalist

Golf is a thoroughly national game; it is as Scotch as haggis, cockie-leekie, high cheekbones, or rowanberry jam

Golf, Lost Leaders (1889)

D H Lawrence (1885-1930), English novelist and poet

You don't know Burns unless you hate the Lockharts and all the estimable bourgeois and upper classes as he did-the narrow-gutted pigeons

From Letter to Donald Carswell (1927)

So this is your Scotland. It is rather nice, but dampish and northern and one shrinks a trifle inside one's skin. For these countries one should be an amphibian

From Letter to Dorothy Brett (August, 1928)

David Livingstone (1813-73), missionary and explorer

No one knows the value of water till he is deprived of it

Private Journals (1851-3)

Men are immortal till their work is done

Letters

I thank God for preserving my life where so many have fallen, and enabling me to do something which I trust will turn out for the true and permanent welfare of Africa

From a letter to his parents and sisters (March, 1856)

The strangest thing I have seen in this country seems really to be broken-heartedness and it attacks free men who have been captured and made slaves

Last Journal of David Livingstone in Central Africa (1874)

Simon Fraser Lovat, Lord (c.1667-1747), Jacobite and clan chief

My dear James, I am going to Heaven, but you must continue to crawl a little longer in this evil world

(April, 1747)
A message from the scaffold to James Fraser, one of his clansmen. Lord Lovat was found guilty of sedition after the disastrous failure of the 1745 rebellion and was condemned to be beheaded

Thomas Babington Macaulay (1st Baron Rothley) (1800-59), English historian and essayist

In the Gaelic tongue Glencoe signifies the Glen of Weeping: and in truth that pass is the most dreary and melancholy of all the Scottish passes, the very Valley of the Shadow of Death

History of England from The Accession of James II (1848-61), Volume 5

Hugh McDiarmid (pseudonym of Christopher Grieve) (1892-1978), poet

There is so much that is bad in all the poetry that Scots people know and admire that it is not surprising that for their pet example of a good bad poet they should have to go outside the range of poetry, good, bad, or indifferent altogether. McGonagall is in a very special category, and has it entirely to himself

Scottish Eccentrics (1936)

George MacDonald (1824-1905), poet and novelist

I do not think the road to contentment lies in despising what we have not got. Let us acknowledge all good, all delight that the world holds, and be content without it

Annals of a Quiet Neighbourhood (1867)

You would not think any duty small if you yourself were great

Willie's Question

George Mackenzie, Sir (1636-91), writer and Lord Advocate

To me it appears undeniable that the Scottish idiom of the British tongue is more fitting for pleading than either the English idiom or the French tongue: for certainly a pleader must use a brisk, smart and quick way of speaking: whereas the English, who are a grave nation, use too slow and grave a pronunciation, and the French a too soft and effeminate one. And therefore I think the English is fit for haranguing, the French for complimenting, but the Scots for pleading

Pleadings in Some Remarkable Cases before the Supreme court of Scotland (1672)

Henry Mackenzie (1745-1831), novelist and essayist

In Scotland we can be very bitter in our Wrath, seldom jocose in our Satire. We can lash an Adversary, but want the Art of laughing at him, which is frequently the severer Revenge of the two

From a letter to his cousin Elizabeth Rose (August, 1774)

Burns, originally virtuous, was seduced by dissipated companions, and after he got into Excise addicted himself to drunkenness, tho' the rays of his genius sometimes broke through the mist of his dissipation: but the habit had got too much power over him to be overcome, and it brought him, with a few lucid intervals, to an early grave

Anecdotes and Egotisms

Charles Rennie McIntosh (1868-1928), architect and designer

Artists (I mean of course Architects) must be as select as those whom they desire to please as those whom they desire to imitate. Without the love of fame they can never do anything excellent: but by an excessive and unsatiable thirst after it they will come to have vulgar views, they will degrade their style and their taste will be corrupted

Untitled Paper on Architecture (c.1892)

Old architecture lived because it had a purpose. Modern architecture, to be real, must not be a mere envelope without contents

Architecture (1893)

Don't meddle with other people's ideas when you have all the work cut out of you in trying to express your own

Seemliness (1902)

James Mackintosh, Sir (1765-1832), philosopher and historian

The accumulation of that power which is conferred by wealth in the hands of the few, is the perpetual source of oppression and neglect to the mass of mankind

Vindiciae Gallicae (1791)

John McLean (1879-1932), revolutionary Marxist

No human being on the face of the earth, no government is going to take from me my right to speak, my right to protest against wrong, my right to do everything that is for the benefit of mankind

A speech given while being tried for sedition in Edinburgh (May, 1918)

Scotland must again have independence, but not to be ruled by traitor kings or chiefs, lawyers and politicians. The communism of the clans must be re-established on a modern basis

All Hail! The Scottish Communist Republic! (August, 1920)

Donald MacLeod (c.1814-57), stonemason and commentator on the Highland Clearances

Sufferings have been inflicted in the Highlands as severe as those occasioned by the policy of the brutal Roman kings in England, deer have extended ranges, while men have been hunted within a narrower and still narrower circle. The strong have fainted in the race for life; the old have been left to die

Gloomy Memories (1857)

Norman MacLeod (1812-72), Church of Scotland minister

People talk of early morning in the country with bleating sheep, singing larks and purling brooks. I prefer the roar which greets my ears when a thousand hammers, thundering on boilers of steam vessels which are to bridge the Atlantic or Pacific, usher in a new day-the type of a new era

Quoted by R Ferguson in George MacLeod, Founder of the Iona Community (1990)

John MacTaggart (1791-1830), writer and folklorist

Once, too, Curiosity dragged me to see the execution of a young man, when in Edinburgh, but she'll drag well if she drags me back again to see such a spectacle. I was not myself, MacTaggart, for a month afterwards, my mind was so disordered with the sight

William MacTaggart (1835-1910), painter

After all, it is not grand scenery that makes a fine landscape. You don't find the best artists working in the Alps. It's the heart that's the thing. You want to express something that appeals to our common humanity, not something extraordinary

John Major (or Mair) (1469-1550), historian and man of letters

It is the food of almost all the inhabitants of Wales, of the northern English (as I learned some seven years back) and of the Scottish peasantry; and yet the main strength of the Scottish and English armies is in men who have been tillers of the soil-a proof that oaten bread is not a thing to be laughed at

On Bread made from Oats, Historia Majoris Britanniae (1521), translated by A Constable (1892) as A History of Greater Britain

Mary Stewart, Mary Queen of Scots (1542-87)

Look to your conscience and remember that the theatre of the world is wider than the realm of England

Said to the commissioners who were appointed to try her (October, 1586), quoted in Mary Queen of Scots (1969), by Antonia Fraser

I die a true woman to my religion, and like a true Scottish woman and a true French woman

Said to Sir James Melville on the morning she was executed (February, 1587)

James Clerk Maxwell
(1831-79), physicist

When at last this little instrument appeared, consisting, as it does, of parts every one of which is familiar to us, and capable of being put together by an amateur, the disappointment arising from its humble appearance was only partially relieved on finding that it was really able to talk

The Telephone (1878)

Either be a machine and see nothing but 'phenomena' or else try to be a man, feeling your life interwoven, as it is, with many others, and strengthened by them whether in life or death

From a letter to R B Litchfield (1879)

Hugh Miller (1802-56), geologist and writer

It was not until I had learned to detect among the ancient sandstone strata of this quarry exactly the same phenomena as those which I used to witness in my walks with Uncle Sandy in the ebb, that I was fairly excited to examine and inquire. It was the necessity which made me a quarrier that taught me to be a geologist

My Schools and Schoolmasters (1854), referring to his first day as an apprentice stonemason

Lord Monboddo (James Burnett) (1714-99), judge and philosopher

There are many in Scotland who call themselves improvers, but who I think are rather *desolators* of the country. Their method is to take into their possession several farms, which no doubt they improve by cultivation. But after they have done so they set them all to one tenant, instead of perhaps five or six who possessed them before

James Graham, Marquis of Montrose (1612-50), soldier and poet, executed by the Covenanters

Let them bestow on ev'ry Airth a Limb:
Open all my Veins, that I may swim
To Thee, My Saviour, in that Crimson Lake;
Then place my pur-boil'd Head upon a Stake;
Scatter my Ashes, throw them in the Air:
Lord (since Thou know'st where all these Atoms are)
I'm hopeful, once Thou'lt recollect my Dust
And confident Thou'lt raise me with the Just

Lines Composed on the Eve of his Execution, known as The Metrical Prayer; published in A Choice Collection of Comic and Serious Scots Poems, both Ancient and Modern (1711) by James Watson

What, am I still a terror to them? Let them look to themselves; my ghost will haunt them

Said in response to the news that an exceptionally strong guard was to be present at his execution (May, 1650); quoted in Montrose (1928) by John Buchan

Alexander Morison, Sir
(1779-1866), physician

Although diseases of the mind do not directly affect the life of the sufferers, they too often deprive them of everything that can render life desirable, and more lasting distress and enduring regret to friends and relatives are occasioned by them than by any other diseased state, or indeed by death itself, which, under such circumstances, is often hailed to be a blessing

Lecture on the Nature, Causes and Treatment of Insanity
Morison was one of the pioneers of psychiatry

John Muir (1838-1914),
naturalist and founder of the
American Natural Park system

Wherever a Scotsman goes, there goes Burns. His grand whole, catholic soul squares with the good of all; therefore we find him in everything everywhere

John of the Mountains (1938), ed. by L M Wolfe

In God's wilderness lies the hope of the world-
the great fresh, unblighted, unredeemed
wilderness. The galling harness of civilization
drops off, and the wounds heal ere we are aware

John of the Mountains (1938), ed. by L M Wolfe

Storms are never counted among the resources
of a country, yet how far they go towards making
brave people

John of the Mountains (1938), ed. by L M Wolfe

Public opinion in a Scotch playground was a
powerful influence in controlling behaviour

The Story of My Boyhood and Youth

The tendency nowadays to wander in wilderness
is delightful to see. Thousands of tired, nerve-
shaken, over-civilized people are beginning to
find out that going to the mountains is going
home; that wilderness is a necessity; and that
mountain parks and reservations are useful not
only as fountains of timber and irrigating rivers,
but as fountains of life

Our National Parks (1901), Chapter 1

The forests of America, however slighted by man, must have been a great delight to God; for they were the best he ever planted

Our National Parks (1901), Chapter 10

James Murray, Sir (1837-1915), lexicographer, first editor of the Oxford English Dictionary

We do not all think alike, walk alike, dress alike, write alike, or dine alike: why should not we use our liberty in speech also, so long as the purpose of speech, to be intelligible, and its grace, are not interfered with?

From a letter to an unnamed recipient (January, 1895)

Charles Neaves, Lord (1800-76), judge, poet and man of letters

Mutton old and claret good were Caledonia's forte,
Before the Southron taxed her drink
and poisoned her with port

*Beef and Potatoes, Songs and Verse: Social and Scientific
(1875)*

John Ogilivie (1579-1615),
Jesuit priest and martyr,
canonized 1976

If the King will be to me as his predecessors were to mine, I will obey and acknowledge him for my King, but if he do otherwise and play the runagate from God, as he and you all do, I will not acknowledge him more than this old hat

Said during his trial for treason (March, 1615)
He was hanged in Glasgow for refusing to take an oath of allegiance to King James VI and I

James Ogilivy, 1st Early of Seafield
(1644-1730), advocate and MP, one of the
negotiators of the Union of Parliaments

Now there's ane end to ane old song

Said on signing the Treaty of Union between Scotland and England in 1707

Margaret Oliphant, Mrs
(1828-97), novelist

To endure hardship and labour demands a kind of heroism-to endure to be useless is the hardest fate of woman

The Melvilles (1852)

A man is none the worse for things that would ruin a girl for ever

Within the Precincts (1879)

Life is no definite thing with a beginning and an end, a growth and a climax; but a basket of fragments, passages that lead to nothing, curious incidents which look of importance at first, but which crumble and break into pieces, dropping into ruins

Review of Henry James's A London Life in Backwoods' Edinburgh Magazine (1888)

Mungo Park
(1771-1806), explorer

I shall set sail for Africa with the fixed resolution
to discover the termination of the Niger or perish
in the attempt

From a letter to Lord Camden (November, 1805)

Thomas Pennant (1726-98),
Welsh naturalist and traveller

The common women are in general most
remarkably plain, and soon acquire an old look,
and by being much exposed to the weather
without hats, such a grin, and contraction of the
muscles, as heightens greatly their natural
hardness of features: I never saw so much
plainness among the lower ranks of females, but
the ne plus ultra of hard features is not found till
you arrive among the fish-women of Aberdeen

A Tour in Scotland in 1769

John Pinkerton (1758-1826),
antiquary and historian

None can more sincerely wish a total extinction of the Scotish *colloquial* dialect than I do, for there are few *modern* Scoticisms which are not barbarisms

Preface to Ancient Scotish Poems (1786)

Allan Ramsay (1686-1758),
poet and bookseller

When these good old Bards wrote, we had not yet made Use of imported Trimmings upon our Cloaths, nor of Foreign Embroidery in our writings. Their Poetry is the Product of their own country, not pilfered and spoiled in the Transportation from abroad. Their images are native, and their Landskips domestick: copied from the Fields and Meadows we every Day behold

Preface to The Ever Green (1724)
The 'Bards' referred to are Dunbar, Henryson and Gavin Douglas

A dish o' married love right soon grows cauld,
And dosens down to nane, as fouk grow auld

The Gentle Shepherd (1725), Act 1 Scene 2

Gie me a lass with a lump of land,
And we for life shall gang thegither;
Tho' daft or wise I'll never demand,
Or black or fair it maks na whether

*The Lass with the Lump of Land from Poems of Allan
Ramsay (1800)*

Allan Ramsay (1713-84),
portrait painter and essayist
(son of the previous entrant)

Lines and colours are of a more determined
nature, and strike the mind more immediately
than words; which, before they can produce any
effect, must be form'd by the mind itself, into
pictures, and consequently require a more
tedious, and more difficult process

On Ridicule (1753)

In every elegant Art, there is a point beyond which rules cannot carry us. Here the deficiency must be supplied by Taste, which will always advantageously distinguish those artists who happen to be blest with it, and perhaps nothing tends more to debase any art, and to render it inelegant, than an attempt to subject any particular Grace in it to a particular Rule

An enquiry into the Principles of English Versification with some analogous remarks upon the versification of the Ancients, an unpublished essay quoted in Poet and Painter: Allan Ramsay, Father and Son (1984) by I G Brown

Marion Reid (née Kirkland) (fl 1843), campaigner for women's rights

No pure and noble-minded woman can long love affectionately, and submit passively to, a vicious and dissipate, or even to a good and virtuous, tyrant without having her own mind greatly deteriorated

A Plea for Woman (1843), Chapter 2

The grand plea for woman sharing with man all the advantages of education is that every rational being is worthy of cultivation, for his own or her own individual sake. The first object in the education of every mind ought to be its own development

A Plea for Woman (1843), Chapter 11

Thomas Reid (1710-96), philosopher, an important exponent of the Common Sense school of philosophy

The belief of a material world is older, and of more authority, than any principles of philosophy. It declines the tribunal of reason, and laughs at all the artillery of the logician

An Inquiry into the Human Mind on the Principles of Common Sense (1764)

There is no greater impediment to the advancement of knowledge than the ambiguity of words

Essays on the Intellectual Powers of Man (1785)

Men are often led into error by the love of simplicity, which disposes us to reduce things to few principles, and to conceive a greater simplicity in nature than there really is

An Inquiry into the Human Mind on the Principles of Common Sense (1764)

William Robertson (1721-93), historian and minister

Thus, during the whole 17th century, the English were gradually refining their language and their taste; in Scotland the former was much debased and the latter almost entirely lost

History of Scotland (1759), Book 8

Dante Gabriel Rossetti (1828-82), English poet

Burns of all poets is the most a Man

On Burns

Samuel Rutherford (1600-61), theologian and Covenanter

I have got summons already before a Superior Judge and Judiciary, and I behove to answer to my first summons, and ere your day come, I will be where few kings and great folks come

Said on his deathbed on hearing that he had been ordered to appear before Parliament on a charge of treason

Walter Scott, Sir (1771-1832), novelist and poet

I do not at all like the task of reviewing and have seldom myself undertaken it-in poetry never-because I am sensible that there is a greater difference in tastes in that department than in any other and that there is much excellent poetry which I am not nowadays able to read without falling asleep

Letter to Anne Seward (November, 1807)

Breathes there the man with soul so dead,
Who never to himself hath said,
This is my own, my native land!
Whose heart hath ne'er within him burned,
As home his footsteps he hath turned
From wandering on a foreign strand!
If such there be, go, mark him well;
For him no Minstrel raptures swell;
High though his titles, proud his name,
Boundless his wealth as wish can claim:
Despite those titles, power, and pelf,
The wretch, concentred all in self,
Living, shall forfeit fair renown,
And doubly dying, shall go down
To the vile dust, from whence he sprung,
Unwept, unhonoured and unsung

The Lay of the Last Minstrel (1805)

O young Lochinvar is come out of the west,
Through all the wide Border his steed was the best;
And save his good broadsword he weapon had none,
He rode all unarmed, and he rode all alone.
So faithful in love, and so dauntless in war,
There never was knight like young Lochinvar

Marmion (1808)

Oh, what a tangled web we weave,
When first we practise to deceive!

Marmion (1808)

The stag at eve had drunk his fill,
Where danced the moon on Monan's rill,
And deep his midnight lair had made
In lone Glenartney's hazel shade

The Lady of the Lake (1810)

I make it a rule to cheat nobody but booksellers,
a race on whom I have no mercy

Letter to Thomas Sheridan (1811)

He that steals a cow from a poor widow, or a
stirk from a cottar, is a thief; he that lifts a drove
from a Sassenach laird, is a gentleman-drover.
And, besides, to take a tree from the forest, a
salmon from the river, a deer from the hill, or a
cow from a lowland strath, is what no Highlander
need ever think shame upon

Waverley (1814)

A lawyer without history or literature is a mechanic, a mere working mason; if he possesses some knowledge of these, he may venture to call himself an architect

Guy Mannering (1815)

To live the life of an author for mere bread is perhaps the most dreadful fate than can be encountered. Booksellers like other men drive the best of bargains they can: with those who have no independent means of support they make them very narrow indeed and sometimes contrive to evade fulfilling them. Besides, they become masters of your time and your labour as well as dictators of the subjects on which they are to be employed...

Letter to James Bailey (June, 1817)

I was not long, however, in making the good discovery, that in order to enjoy leisure it is absolutely necessary it should be preceded by occupation

The Monastery (1820)

The hour's come, but not the man

The Heart of Midlothian (1818)

We had better remain in union with England, even at the risk of becoming a subordinate species of Northumberland, as far as national consequence is concerned, than remedy ourselves by even hinting the possibility of a rupture. But there is no harm in wishing Scotland to have just so much ill-nature, according to her own proverb, as may keep her good-nature from being abused

Letters of Malachi Malagrowther on the Proposed Change of Currency (1826)

Scotland, completely liberalised, as she is in a fair way of being, will be the most dangerous neighbour to England that she has had since 1639. There is yet time to make a stand, for there is yet a great deal of good and genuine feeling left in the country. But if you *unscotch* us you will find us damned mischievous Englishmen

Letter to J W Croker (March, 1826)

Many a clever boy is flogged into a dunce and many an original composition corrected into mediocrity

Journal (June, 1826)

But who cares for the whipped cream of London society?

Journal (April, 1828)

Among all the provinces in Scotland, if an intelligent stranger were asked to describe the most varied and the most beautiful, it is probable he would name the county of Perth

The Fair Maid of Perth (1828)

To the Lords of Convention, 'twas Claverhouse spoke
Ere the King's crown shall fall there are crowns to be broke
So let each Cavalier who loves honour and me,
Come follow the bonnet of Bonny Dundee

The Doom of Devorgoil, Bonny Dundee (1830)

London licks the butter of our bread by opening a better market for ambition

Journal (March, 1829)

Come fill up my cup, come fill up my can,
Come saddle your horses, and call up your men;
Come open your gates, and let me gae free,
For it's up with the bonnets of Bonny Dundee!

The Doom of Devorgoil, Bonny Dundee (1830)

Surely chess-playing is a sad waste of brains

Memoirs of the Life of Walter Scott (1837-8) by J G Lockhart

Patrick Sellar (1780-1851), lawyer and estate factor on the estate of the 1st Duke of Sutherland

I was at once a convert to the principle now almost universally acted on in the Highlands of Scotland, viz that the people should be employed in securing the natural riches of the sea-coast; that the mildew of the interior should be allowed to fall upon grass, and not upon corn; and that several hundred miles of Alpine plants, flourishing in these districts, in curious succession at all seasons, and out of the reach of anything but sheep, be converted into wood and mutton for the English manufacturer

Quoted in The Trial of Patrick Sellar (1962) by Ian Grimble

William Shakespeare (1564-1616), English playwright and poet

If that you will France win
Then with Scotland first begin

Henry V, Act 1 Scene 2

King Henry: We do not mean the coursing snatchers only,
But fear the main intendment of the Scot,
Who hath been still a giddy neighbour to us;
For you shall read, that my great-grandfather
Never went with his forces into France,
But that the Scot on his unfurnish'd kingdom
Came pouring, like the tide into a breach

Henry V, Act 1 Scene 1

Macduff: Stands Scotland where it did?
Ross: Alas poor country!
Almost afraid to know itself. It cannot
Be call'd our mother, but our grave: where nothing,
But who knows nothing, is once seen to smile;
Where sighs, and groan, and shrieks that rent the air,
Are made, not mark'd ; where violent sorrow seems
A modern ecstasy

Macbeth, Act 4 Scene 3

James Scott Skinner (1843-1927), fiddler and composer

The reel should be played crisp and birly like a weel-gaun wheelie

George Bernard Shaw (1856-1950), Irish playwright

God help England if she had no Scots to think for her!

The Apple Cart, Act 2 (1929)

James Young Simpson, Sir (1811-70), obstetrician

I feel that the greater the good I can accomplish for my profession and humanity, the greater will always be the temporary blame attempted to be heaped on me by the bigoted portion of the profession

Quoted in Sir James Y Simpson (1896) by E B Simpson
Simpson faced a lot of criticism and opposition in his efforts to relieve the pain of childbirth because this was regarded as quite natural and in line with the Scriptures

Adam Skirving
(1719-1803), songwriter

Hey, Johnnie Cope, are ye waukin', yet?
Or are your drums a-beating yet?
If ye were waukin' I wad wait
Tae gang tae the coals I, the mornin'

Johnnie Cope Skirving was a Jacobite and the song was written to celebrate the Battle of Prestonpans (1745)

Mary Slessor
(1848-1915), missionary

What a strange thing is sympathy. Undefinable, untranslatable, and yet the most real thing and the greatest power in human life. How strangely how souls leap out to other souls without our choosing or knowing why. The man or woman who possesses this subtle gift possesses the most precious thing on earth

Quoted in The Expendable Mary Slessor (1980) by James Buchan

Everybody drinks. I have lain down at night, knowing that not a sober man and hardly a sober woman was within miles of me

A reference to the alcohol problem of the Okoyong people quoted in The Expendable Mary Slessor (1980) by James Buchan

Money is something I do not understand because I've never had to deal with it. What's money to God?

Quoted in The Expendable Mary Slessor (1980) by James Buchan

Samuel Smiles (1812-1904), social reformer and moralist

The spirit of self-help is the root of all genuine growth in the individual

Self-help (1859)

Self-respect is the noblest garment with which a man may clothe himself—the most elevating feeling with which the mind can be inspired

Self-help (1859)

A place for everything and everything in its place

Thrift (1875)

That terrible Nobody! How much has he to answer for. More mischief is done by Nobody than by all the world besides

Thrift (1875)

'It will do!' is the common phrase of those who neglect little things. 'It will do!' has blighted many a character, blasted many a fortune, burnt down many a house, sunk many a ship, and irretrievably ruined thousands of hopeful projects of human good

Thrift (1875)

Adam Smith (1723-90), economist and philosopher

It is not from the benevolence of the butcher, the brewer, or the baker, that we expect our dinner, but from their regard to their own interest

An Inquiry into the Nature and Causes of the Wealth of Nations (1776)

People of the same trade seldom meet together, even for merriment and diversion, but the conversation ends in a conspiracy against the public, or in some contrivance to raise prices

An Inquiry into the Nature and Causes of the Wealth of Nations (1776)

The man whose whole life is spent in performing a few simple operations, of which the effects are, perhaps, always the same, or very nearly the same, has no occasion to exert his understanding, or to exercise his invention in finding out expedients for removing difficulties which never occur. He naturally loses, therefore, the habit of such exertion, and generally becomes as stupid and ignorant as it is possible for a human creature to become

An Inquiry into the Nature and Causes of the Wealth of Nations (1776)

Alexander Smith
(1830-67), poet

City! I am true son of thine:
Ne'er dwelt I where great mornings shine
Around the bleating pens;
Ne'er by the rivulets I strayed,
And ne'er upon my childhood weighed
The silence of the glens,
Instead of shores where ocean beats
I hear the ebb and flow of streets

Glasgow, City Poems (1857)

A sacredness of love and death
Dwells in thy noise and smoky breath

Glasgow, City Poems (1857)

It is not of so much consequence what you say, as how you say it. Memorable sentences are memorable on account of some single irradiating word

On the Writing of Essays, Dreamthorp (1863)

A man gazing on the stars is proverbially at the mercy of the puddles on the road

Men of Letters, Dreamthorp (1863)

Stirling, like a huge brooch, clasps Highlands and Lowlands together

A Summer in Skye (1865)

Sydney Smith (1771-1845), English writer and co-founder of the Edinburgh Review

I look upon Switzerland as a sort of inferior Scotland

From a letter to Lord Holland, quoted in Letters of Sydney Smith (1953), edited by N C Smith

It requires a surgical operation to get a joke well into a Scottish understanding

Quoted in A Memoir of the Reverend Sydney Smith (1855) by Lady Holland

We cultivate literature on a little oatmeal

*Proposed motto for the Edinburgh Review, but considered
'too near the truth to be admitted'; quoted in A Memoir of
the Reverend Sydney Smith (1855) by Lady Holland*

When shall I see Scotland again? Never shall I
forget the happy days I passed there, amidst
odious smells, barbarian sounds, bad suppers,
excellent hearts, and most enlightened and
cultivated understanding

*Letter to Francis Jeffrey (March, 1814); quoted in A Memoir
of the Reverend Sydney Smith (1855) by Lady Holland*

Tobias Smollett
(1721-71), novelist

Resentment of my country's fate
Within my filial breast shall beat;
And, spite of the insulting foe,
My sympathizing verse shall flow,
Mourn, hapless Caledonia, mourn
Thy banish'd peace, thy laurels torn

*The Tears of Scotland (1746)
Written after the Battle of Culloden*

London is the devil's drawing-room

The Adventures of Roderick Random (1748)

I consider the world as made for me, not me for the world. It is my Maxim therefore to enjoy it while I can, and let futurity shift for itself

The Adventures of Roderick Random (1748)

Edinburgh is a hot-bed of genius

The Expedition of Humphry Clinker (1771)

In the fields, called Links, the citizens of Edinburgh divert themselves at a game called golf, in which they use a curious kind of bats tipped with horn and small elastic balls of leather, stuffed with feathers, less than tennis balls, but of much harder consistency: this they strike with such force and dexterity from one hole to another that they will fly to an incredible distance

The Expedition of Humphry Clinker (1771)

Mary Somerville (née Fairfax) (1780-1872), mathematician and writer

In our play-hours we amused ourselves with playing at ball, marbles, and especially at 'Scotch and English', a game which represented a raid on the debatable land, or Border between Scotland and England, in which each party tried to rob the other of their playthings. The little ones always compelled to be English, for the bigger girls thought it too degrading

From Personal Recollections from Early Life to Old Age of Mary Somerville (1873)

A man can always command his time under the plea of business, a woman is not allowed such an excuse

From Personal Recollections from Early Life to Old Age of Mary Somerville (1873)

Charles Hamilton Sorley
(1895-1915), poet

Earth that blossom'd and was glad
'Neath the cross that Christ had,
Shall rejoice and blossom too
When the bullet reaches you

Untitled Poem

When you see millions of the mouthless dead
Across your dreams in pale battalions go,
Say not soft things as other men have said
That you'll remember. For you need not so
Give them praise. For deaf, how should they know
It is not curses heaped on each gashed head?
Nor tears. Their blind eyes see not your tears flow
Nor honour. It is easy to be dead

Marlborough and other poems (1916)
Sorley was killed in a action in 1915

William Soutar
(1896-1943), poet

Life is no loving father, but a force with which
we must contend and to which we must adapt
the self

Diary entry (June, 1932)

Stair, 1st Earl of (Sir John Dalrymple)
(1648-1707), judge and Secretary of
State, held responsible for the
Massacre of Glencoe

The McDonalds will fall in this net. That's the
only popish clan in the kingdom, and it will be
popular to take severe course with them. Let me
hear from you with the first whether you think
this is the proper season to maul them in the cold
long nights, and what force will be necessary

*From a letter to Lt. Col. Hamilton at Fort William
(December, 1691)*

Just now, my Lord Argyll tells me that Glencoe hath not taken the oaths, at which I rejoice. It's a great work of charity to be exact in rooting out that damnable sept, the worst in all the Highlands

From a letter to Sir Thomas Livingston (January 1692) written on receiving the news that the chief of the Glencoe McDonalds had left it too late to take the required oath of loyalty to the King

Robert Louis Stevenson (1850-94), novelist, poet and essayist

For my own part, I travel not to go anywhere, but to go. I travel for travel's sake

Travels with a Donkey (1879)

Marriage is terrifying, but so is a cold and forlorn old age

Virginibus Puerisque (1881)

[…] even if we take marriage at its lowest, even if we regard it as no more than a sort of friendship recognized by the police […]

Virginibus Puerisque (1881)

Lastly (and this is, perhaps, the golden rule) no man should ever marry a teetotaller or a man who does not smoke

Virginibus Puerisque (1881)

You can read Kant by yourself if you wanted, but you must share a joke with someone else

Virginibus Puerisque (1881)

The cruellest lies are often told in silence. A man may have sat in a room for hours and not opened his teeth, and yet come out of that room a disloyal friend and a vile calumnator

Virginibus Puerisque (1881)

Books are good enough in their own way, but they are a mighty bloodless substitute for life

Virginibus Puerisque (1881)

To travel hopefully is a better thing than to arrive

Virginibus Puerisque (1881)

It is better to lose health like a spendthrift than to waste it like a miser. It is better to live and be done with it than to die daily in the sick room

Virginibus Puerisque (1881)

We are in such haste to be doing, to be writing, to be gathering gear, to make our voice audible a moment in the derisive silence of eternity, that we forget that one thing, of which these are but parts-namely to live

Virginibus Puerisque (1881)

Scotland is indefinable; it has no unity except upon the map

The Silverado Squatters (1883)

And though I would rather die elsewhere, yet in my heart of hearts I long to be buried among good Scots clods

The Silverado Squatters (1883)

Sight-seeing is the art of disappointment

The Silverado Squatters (1883)

But somehow life is warmer and closer; the heart burns more redly; the lights of home shine softer on the rainy streets; the very names, endeared in verse and music, cling nearer round our hearts

The Silverado Squatters (1883); referring to life in Scotland, as opposed to England

A child should always say what's true,
And speak when he is spoken to,
And behave mannerly at table:
At least as far as he is able

Whole Duty of Children from A Child's Garden of Verses (1885)

The first step for all is to learn to the very dregs our own ignoble fallibility

Memories and Portraits (1887)

Faith means holding the same opinions as the person employing the word

Memories and Portraits (1887)

Marriage is one long conversation, chequered by disputes

Memories and Portraits (1887)

Scientific men, who imagine that their science affords an answer to the problem of existence, are perhaps the most to be pitied of mankind; and contemned

Memories and Portraits (1887)

For that is the mark of the Scot of all classes; that he stands in an attitude towards the past unthinkable to Englishman, and remembers and cherishes the memory of his forebears good and bad; and there burns alive in him a sense of identity with the dead even to the twentieth generation

Weir of Hermiston, published posthumously in 1896

The bourgeoisie's weapon is starvation. If as an artist or writer you run counter to their narrow notions they simply and silently withdraw your means of substance

Quoted in The Death of Stevenson by Lloyd Osbourne, preface to the Tusitala edition of Weir of Hermiston (1924)

Charles Edward Stewart, Prince (Bonnie Prince Charlie, The Young Pretender) (1720-88), claimant to the throne

Let what will happen, the stroke is struck and I have taken a firm resolution to conquer or die and to stand my ground as long as I have a man remaining with me

From a letter to his father, James Stewart, the Old Pretender, (1745)

When I came to Scotland I knew well enough what to expect from my enemies, but I little foresaw what I meet from my friends

From a letter to Lord George Murray in response to criticisms of his leadership (January, 1746)

James Stewart (The Old Pretender) 1688-1766, claimant to the throne

If I had been acquainted with it in time, I had certainly done my best to prevent its being executed. If it was rash, I cannot but say it was a bold undertaking, and the courage and sentiments the Prince expresses on this occasion will always do him honour

From a letter to the Earl Marischal (1745) on the landing in Scotland of Prince Charles Edward

Jonathon Swift (1667-1745), Anglo-Irish satirist and clergyman

This I have observed more frequently among the Scots than any other nation, who are very careful not to omit the minutest circumstances of time or place; which kind of discourse, if it were not a little relieved by the uncouth terms and phrases, as well as accent and gesture peculiar to that country, would be hardly tolerable

Hints towards an Essay on Conversation; he is here commenting on people who 'relate facts of no consequence'

William Thom
(1798-1848), poet

The motherless bairn gangs till his lane bed,
Nane covers his cauld back, or haps his bare head;
His wee hackit heelies are hard as the airn,
An litheless the lair o' the mitherless bairn!

The Mitherless Bairn (c.1841)

Thomas the Rhymer (Thomas of Ercildoune) (c.1220-97), seer

The Burn o Breid
Sall rin fu reid

A prophecy attributed to Thomas the Rhymer which has been interpreted as referring to the Battle of Bannockburn

The teeth of the sheep shall lay the plough on the shelf

A prophecy attributed to Thomas the Rhymer which has been interpreted as referring to the Highland Clearances

James Thomson
(1700-48), poet

When Britain first, at heaven's command,
Arose from out the azure main,
This was the charter of the land,
And guardian angels sung this strain:
'Rule Britannia, rule the waves:
Britons never will be slaves.'

Alfred: a Masque (1740)

James Thomson (BV)
(1834-82), poet and journalist

Give a man a pipe he can smoke,
Give a man a book he can read;
And his home is bright with a calm delight,
Though the rooms be poor indeed

Sunday up the River (1869)

The city is of Night, but not of Sleep:
There sweet Sleep is not for the weary brain:
The pitiless hours like years and ages creep,
A night seems termless hell

The City of Dreadful Night (1874)

John Thomson (1837-1921), photographer, writer and traveller

The camera should be a power in this age of instruction for the instruction of the age

(1875)

Turgot (c.1060-c.1115), Anglo-Saxon monk, confessor to St Margaret

The Queen united such strictness to her sweetness and such sweetness to her strictness that all who were in her service, men as well as women, while fearing her loved and while loving her feared her

The Life of St Margaret, Queen of Scotland

He stood there in a strait, with everything against him; whither to know he knew not. He had come to announce to his mother that his father and brother had been slain, and he found his mother, whom he loved most dearly, at the point of death. Whom to lament first he knew not

Written of Edgar's arrival at Queen Margaret's deathbed in The Life of St Margaret, Queen of Scotland

Queen Victoria (1819-1901)

There is a great peculiarity about the Highlands and the Highlanders; and they are such a chivalrous, fine, active people

Our Life in the Highlands (1868)

The impression Edinburgh has made on me is very great; it is quite beautiful, totally unlike anything else I have ever seen: and what is even more, Albert, who has seen so much, says it is unlike anything he ever saw

Letters

William Wallace (c.1270-1305) Scottish patriot, Guardian of Scotland from 1298

I resolved to spare no strain to drive out of this kingdom every single Englishman and had I not been met at every turn by the opposition of our nobles, 'tis beyond a doubt that I would have done it

Attributed to Wallace after the defeat at Falkirk (July, 1298) in an exchange with Robert Bruce, quoted in Historia Majoris Britanniae by John Major (1469-1550), translated by A Constable (1892)

I tell you truly, liberty is the best of things; never live under the halter of slavery

A maxim traditionally associated with Wallace

James Watt (1736-1819), engineer and inventor

I was thinking upon the engine at the time, and had gone as far as the Herd's house when the idea came into my mind, that as steam was an elastic body, it would rush into a vacuum, and, if a communication was made between the cylinder and the exhausted vessel, it would rush into it, and might there be condensed without cooling the cylinder

Quoted in James Watt, Craftsman and Engineer (1935) by H W Dickinson
Referring to the moment when he had the idea of having a separate steam condenser in a steam engine

I think that I shall not long have anything to do with the House of Commons again—I never saw so many wrong-headed people on all sides gathered together

Letter to his wife (1767)

David Wilkie, Sir
(1785-1841), artist

The use of art to memory can never be doubted by any intelligent being. That which conveys ideas, forms and appearances, clear and distinct, when language is lost or unintelligible, which speaks all tongues, living or dead, polite or barbarous, proclaims its own usefulness

John Witherspoon (1723-94), minister who emigrated to America, later becoming President of the College of New Jersey (now Princeton University)

I willingly embrace the opportunity of declaring my opinion without hesitation that the cause in which America is now in arms is the cause of justice and liberty

From a sermon given at Princeton (May, 1776)
He helped to frame the American Declaration of Independence (4 July, 1776)

Dorothy Wordsworth (1771-1855), English writer and sister of William Wordsworth

Scotland is the country above all others that I have seen, in which a man of imagination may carve out his own pleasures; there are so many *inhabited* solitudes

Recollections of a Tour made in Scotland AD 1803 (1874)

William Wordsworth (1770-1850), English poet

I mourned with thousands, but as one
More deeply grieved, for he was gone
Whose lights I hailed when first it shone,
And showed my youth
How verse may build a princely throne
On humble truth
At the Grave of Burns

SCOTTISH SAYINGS AND PROVERBS

HEALTH

A cauld needs the cook as muckle as the doctor

A cold can be cured by nutritious food as effectively as by medicine

Better wear shoon than sheets

It is better to wear shoes to keep the feet warm and dry, even though this may be expensive, rather than become ill

Feed a cauld and starve a fever

Indicating that the traditional advice to give invalids nutritious food is not always appropriate, especially if they are suffering from feverish illnesses

Feed a cauld but hunger a colic

A similar sentiment to the previous saying except that the condition not requiring nutritious food is a stomach disorder

Fill fu' and haud fu' maks a stark man

Plenty of good food and drink makes a person strong

Gae tae bed wi' the lamb and rise wi' the laverock

A recipe for remaining healthy, a Scots version of 'early to bed, early to rise'

He that eats but ae dish seldom needs the doctor

A warning to be sparing in the amount of food which you eat, if you want to remain healthy

If ye want to be soon weel be lang sick

Not a recommendation to malinger, but advice not to get out of bed too soon after you have been ill

Licht suppers mak lang days

A recommendation to eat sparingly, especially in the evening, if you wish to live to an old age

Rise when the day daws,
Bed when the nicht fa's

Another injunction to stay healthy by going to bed early and getting up early

Suppers kill mair than doctors cure

Another recommendation to eat sparingly, especially in the evening

FOOD

A drap and a bit's but sma' requite

Said as an invitation to guests to partake of food and drink, indicating that this is little recompense for their friendship

A hungry man's an angry man

This speaks for itself—and it is undoubtedly true that many people become bad-tempered when they get hungry

A hungry man's meat is lang o' makin' ready

When you are very hungry the preparation of your food seems to take a very long time, a similar saying to 'the watched pot never boils'

A hungry wame has nae lugs

Those who are hungry seem to have lost the power of hearing and so don't listen to reason

A kiss and a drink o' watter mak a wersh breakfast

Said as a warning to a couple who think that they can live on love and very little else

As the soo fills, the draff soors

Literally, as the sow fills up, its food begins to taste sour, but used as a compliment to a host, indicating that the food has been so plentiful and so good, that the guest's appetite has gone and he/she can eat no more

Bannocks are better than nae breid

Very plain food is better than no food at all, a similar saying to 'half a loaf is better than no bread'

Better belly burst than gude meat spoil

It is better to eat too much than let good food go to waste, said by those who eat too much, as justification for their greed

Better wait on the cook than the doctor

A reference to the fact that many people felt that nourishing food was more important to the ill than medicine, although this could vary with the type of illness

Breid's hoose is skailed never

You can never say of a house that contains bread that it has no food in it

Eat in measure and defy the doctor

Moderation in eating makes for a healthy life

Eats meat, and never fed; wears claes and never cled

No matter how well-fed or well-clothed some people may be, they never seem to look any better for this

Eat weel's drink weel's brither

Eating well and drinking well should go together

Fat paunches bode lean pows

People who are greedy and over-fed have empty heads

Hunger's good kitchen

When you're hungry any food tastes good

Hunger's good kitchen to a cauld potato, but a wet divot to the lowe o' love

Hunger makes the humblest of food, such as a cold potato, seem very appetizing, but it damps down romantic passion

I'm neither sma' drink thirsty nor grey bread hungry

Used by someone who is disappointed at the standard of fare which he/she has been offered by a host

Mennans are better than nae meat

Both this and the next saying indicate that it is better to have very little food than no food at all. In Scots the word meat is often used for food generally and mennans are minnows or very small fish

Mennans are better than nae fish

See the saying above

Naething sooner maks a man auld-like than fitting ill to his meat

Nothing ages people so rapidly as being ill-fed

Ne'er gie' me death in a toom dish

A jocular saying used by people who like their food and want some of it, literally meaning don't give me death by means of an empty dish, don't starve me to death

Ne'er speak ill o' them whose breid ye eat

A warning not to criticize your host

O' a' the meat in the warld, the drink gaes best doon

This speaks for itself in a land which makes and loves whisky

Poor folk seek meat for their stamacks and rich folk seek stamacks for their meat

The poor eat because they're hungry, the rich because they feel they have to, even if they have little appetite

Some hae meat and canna eat
And some wad meat that want it;
But we hae meat and we can eat,
For which the Lord be thankit

A grace said before meals, known as the Selkirk Grace

Stuffin' hauds oot storms

Advice given to people who are setting out on a journey in bad weather to eat well before they leave

Tak a piece-your teeth's longer than your beard

Words of encouragement said to children to get them to take a titbit or treat while they have the chance

The nearer the grave, the greedier

The older people get, the more food they like to have

They hae need o' a canny cook that hae but ae egg to their denner

It takes a clever, ingenious cook to make a meal out of very little, also extended to mean that it takes a resourceful person to make the most of what is to hand

They may ken by your beard what has been on your board

A way of telling someone that he has some of the food which he has just eaten on his beard or chin

Welcome's the best dish in the kitchen

Food given with a good will tastes the best

What's in your wame's no in your testament

Said as an encouragement to someone to eat up, a reminder that if you eat everything on your plate you cannot leave it to someone else in your will

When all fruit fa's, welcome ha's

When we have consumed all the finer food, we must be content with the plain kind

Ye hae tint your ain stamack an' found a tyke's

A remark made to someone who is eating a great deal, as though very hungry

Your meat will mak you bonny and when you're bonny you'll be well lo'ed and when you're well lo'ed you'll be licht-hearted and when you're licht-hearted you'll loup far

Said to children as encouragement to them to eat

WEATHER

About the moon there is a brough,
The weather will be cold and rough

A warning of rough weather if there is a halo effect round the moon

A green Yule maks a fat kirkyard

A wet winter results in many deaths, because of the many illnesses that are caused or worsened by damp conditions

As the day lengthens, the cauld strengthens

A reminder that, when the days begin to get longer, at the beginning of the year, the weather is often colder than, say, in November and December

Cast not a clout till May be oot

Often taken to mean that people should not remove any of their winter clothing until the month of May has finished, but May is thought by some to refer to the hawthorn, the advice being not to remove any winter clothes until the hawthorn is in blossom

East and wast the sign o' a blast; north and south,
the sign o' a drouth

*A weather saying using the direction of the prevailing wind
as a predictor*

E'ening grey an' a morning red, put on your hat
or ye'll wet your head.
E'ening red an' a morning grey, is a taiken o' a
bonny day

*A weather saying meaning much the same as 'red sky in the
morning, shepherd's warning, red sky at night, shepherd's
delight'*

If Candlemas Day be dry and fair
The hauf o' winter's to come and mair,
If Candlemas Day be wet and foul,
The hauf o winter's gaun at Yule

*Candlemas Day is February 2 and it was taken as a good
weather sign if it was wet then*

If grass grows green in Janaveer,
It will be the waur for it a' the year

*The idea was that the grass was green too early in the year
for survival*

Mist in May and heat in June make the harvest right soon

A self-evident weather saying

Mony haws, mony snaws

A warning that a good harvest of haw berries will result in a cold, hard winter

Sorrow an' ill weather come unca'd

Both ill fortune and ill weather are beyond our control

The rain cams scouth, when the wind's i' the south

In this context scouth means freely, without restraint, and so the saying indicates that heavy rain will occur when there is a wind blowing from the south

Under water dearth, under snaw bread

A field that has been flooded with water will produce a very poor crop, but one that has been covered in snow will produce a good one

When the moon is on her back
Gae mend your shoon and sort your thack

When the moon seems to be in such a position, it should be seen as a sign of rain and appropriate measures taken

MONEY

A' complain o' want o' siller, but nane o' want o' sense

A saying indicating that desiring more money is a much commoner human preoccupation than desiring more sense

A deaf man will hear the clink o' money

A saying emphasizing very well the lure of money

A fu' sack can bear a clout i' the side

A prosperous person can afford to take a few knocks from fate

Better a tocher in her than wi' her

A tocher was a woman's dowry and this saying suggests that it was better for a woman to have good qualities within rather than to have a lot of money and possessions

Eaten meat is ill to pay

No-one likes to have to pay for something that has already been consumed

Gathering gear is weel-liket wark

Acquiring money is generally thought to be a pleasant occupation

Get what you can, and keep what you hae, that's the way to get rich

It sounds so easy that it makes you wonder why there are not more rich people around!

He's got his nose in a gude kail pat

Said of someone who has married someone well-off, literally he has got his head in a good soup pot

He wad rake hell for a bodle

A saying indicating how much someone loves money and what a miser he is, a bodle being an old copper coin

He wad skin a louse for the tallow

A saying used to describe just how miserly someone is

It's as easy to get siller frae a lawyer as butter frae a black dog's hause

Hause here means throat and so you get a pretty good idea of how difficult the speaker considered such a task to be

It's folly to live poor to dee rich

The moral is self-evident, akin to 'you can't take it with you'

Lay your wame to your winning

A warning not to consume more than you can afford

Moyen does muckle, but money does mair

Influence can do a lot, but money is even more powerful

Put twa pennies in a purse and they will creep thigither

A saying indicating how money soon accumulates if you save it

There are nane sae weel shod but may slip

Everyone, including the wealthy, run the risk of mishap

The siller penny slays mair souls than the nakit sword slays bodies

A comment on the destructive power of money

Want o' wit is waur than want o' gear

It is worse to be lacking in intelligence and sense than to be lacking in money

Wealth gars wits waver

People tend to lose their commonsense when money is involved

Wealth has made mair men covetous than covetousness has made men wealthy

A warning against greed

SILENCE

A close mou catches nae flees

A recommendation to say as little as possible, a variation on 'shut your mouth and you'll get no flies'

Ah dinna bile ma cabbages twice

Said as a refusal to repeat what has just been said, literally 'I don't boil my cabbages twice'

Dinna open yer mou tae fill ither fowks

A warning not to gossip

Gie yer tongue mair holidays than yer heid

An imaginative way of suggesting that people should think more than they say

He that spares to speak, spares to speed

For once a saying not in favour of silence, but one which suggests that people who don't point out their own talents don't succeed

Keep your breath tae cool yer parritch

A piece of advice given to someone who is wasting words

Keep yer gab steekit when ye kenna yer company

A warning not to say too much in front of strangers, literally to keep your mouth closed when you don't know who is present

Keep yer mou shut and yer een open

A warning that you will learn more if you say little and observe a lot

Pint stoups hae lang lugs

A reminder that those who drink too much often say too much

Put your thoom on that!

Literally put your thumb on that, said as a warning to keep something secret

The loodest bummer's no the best bee

The person who says the most is rarely the most effective person

Think mair than ye say

Devote more time to thought than speech

Wae is the wife that wants a tongue, but weel's the man that gat her

It is unfortunate to be a woman who says very little, since little notice will be taken of her, but it is fortunate to be a man who marries such a woman

When a' men speak, nae man hears

If everyone speaks at once, no-one hears or takes in anything that is said

Wide lugs and a short tongue are best

It is best to listen a lot and say very little

TRUTH

A fu' heart never lied

People are more likely to tell the truth when they are in the grip of emotion

Auld saws speak truths

There's a lot of truth in old sayings, as this collection proves

Craft maun hae claes, but truth gangs nakit

Cunning may be disguised, but truth does not need any cover or embellishment

Facts are chiels that winna ding

Facts, and therefore the truth, cannot be denied

He never lies, but when the holly's green

Since holly is an evergreen tree, this saying indicates that the person in question never tells the truth

If a'thing's true, that's nae lee

A saying used to express disbelief in what has just been said

It's a sin to lee on the diel

You should always speak the truth, even when wicked people are concerned

Truth and honesty keep the croon on the causey

People who are honest and truthful stay out of trouble. The 'croon o' the cause' or the crown of the causeway was the highest part of the street, farthest way from the gutter where all the rubbish gathered

Truth will stand when a'thing's failin'

Truth can be relied upon when everything else fails

WORDS

A' are no freens that speak us fair

Just because someone pays you a compliment or says something nice about you, you cannot assume that he/she is your friend

A' his buzz shaks nae barley

Said of someone who may say a great deal but whose words have no effect on the situation

A man o' words but no' o' deeds is like a garden fu' o' weeds

A picturesque way of saying that actions are much more useful than mere words

Bairns speak i' the field whit they hear i' the ha'

A warning to parents to be careful what they say in front of the children as they may well repeat this outside

Bees that hae honey in their mouths hae stings in their tails

A warning to be wary of people who are particularly eloquent or flattering, as they may be up to no good

Fair words winna mak the pot boil

A saying stressing the inadequacy of mere words

Glib i' the tongue is aye glaikit at the heart

Another saying warning against being impressed or taken in by eloquent or flattering people, as they are very likely to be insincere

It's a gude tongue that says nae ill, but a better heart that thinks none

A self-evident saying praising the harbouring of charitable thoughts

Muckle spoken, part spilt

Said of a topic about which so much has been said, that much of this has been lost or ignored

Praise without profit puts little i' the pot

Fine words alone are not much practical use to anyone

Sticks and stanes may brak my banes, But names will never hurt me

A saying indicating that, although physical abuse may do harm to someone, verbal insults will not, often used by schoolchildren to their tormentors

Thanks winna feed the cat

Verbal thanks is not worth much, sometimes said as a grudging, belittling acknowledgement of spoken thanks

There's a word in my wame, but it's o'er far down

A saying used by someone to indicate that he/she cannot think of the right word at that moment, similar to a word on the tip of one's tongue

Words are but wind, but dunts are the devil

Blows are much worse than verbal abuse

Ye wad wheedle a laverock frae the lift

Said to someone who is particularly charming or persuasive, as though able to persuade the lark to leave the sky

GLOSSARY OF SCOTS WORDS

a'	all
aboon	above
acquent	acquainted
ae	one
afore	before
aft	often
agley	awry, wrong
ah	I
airm	arm
airn	iron
airth	point of the compass, direction
an'	and
auld	old
bairn	child
bane	bone
bannock	an unleavened cake
beld	bald
bien	comfortable
bile	boil
bonie, bony	bonny
breid	bread

brent	smooth, unwrinkled
brither	brother
bummer	a creature that makes a buzzing noise, a bee
canna	cannot
canny	careful
canty	lively
cauld	cold
chiel	a young man, a fellow
claes	clothes
cled	clad
clout	cloth
croon	crown
dee	die
denner	dinner
diel	devil
ding	deal blows, defeat
dinna	don't
doon	down
dosen	become numb
draff	pig-food
drap	drop
drouth	drought, thirst
dunt	blow

een	eyes
fa'	fall, befall
flee	fly
fowk	folk
frae	from
freen	friend
fu'	full
gab	mouth
gae	go
gang	go
gar	make, cause to
gaun	going
gear	wealth
gie	give
giftie	gift
glaikit	foolish, stupid
gree	agree
bear the gree	be the victor, be supreme
greet	cry
gude	good
guid	good
ha'	hall
hack	a crack in the skin
hackit	having

hae	have
hamely	homely
hap	cover
har'sts	harvests
haud	hold
hauf	half
hause	throat
heid	head
het	hot
i'	in
ither	other
ithers	others
Janaveer	January
kail	soup; kale
kenna	don't know
kennin'	a little bit
kirk	church
lane	solitary, lonely
lane, thy lane	alone, on your own
lang	long
laverock	lark
lee	lie, to tell lies
lift	sky
licht	light

lo'ed	loved
loodest	loudest
lowe	flame
lowp	leap
lug	ear
mair	more
mak	make
maun	must
meat	food
mennan	minnow
monie, mony	many
mou	mouth
moyen	influence
muckle	much, large
nae	no
naething	nothing
nakit	naked
nane	none
nicht	night
no'	not
o'	of
orsels	ourselves
oot	out
parritch	porridge

pat	pot
piece	a piece of bread, a sandwich
poortith	poverty
pow	head
prent	print
pudden	pudding
reid	red
rin	run
sall	shall
shak	shake
shoon	shoes
siller	silver
simmer	summer
skail	empty, spill
sma'	small
snaw	snow
sonsie	plump
soo	sow
soor	sour
stamack	stomach
stark	strong
steekit	closed
stoup	flagon, jug
tae	to

taiken	token
tak	take
thack	thatch
thankit	thanked
thigither	together
thoom	thumb
tint	lost
toom	empty
tyke	dog
unca'd	uncalled
wad	would
wame	stomach
wark	work
warld	world
wast	west
watter	water
waur	worse
weel	well
wersh	tasteless
wham	whom
whit	what
winna	won't
wordy	worthy
wrang	wrong

THE
CONCISE DICTIONARY
OF

SCOTTISH
WORDS AND
PHRASES

BETTY KIRKPATRICK

1-905102-88-7, £4.99

If you have enjoyed this book,
please see others like it on
www.crombiejardine.com

All Crombie Jardine books are available from High
Street bookshops, Amazon or Bookpost
(P.O. Box 29, Douglas, Isle of Man, IM99 1BQ.
Tel: 01624 677237, Fax: 01624 670923,
Email: bookshop@enterprise.net.
Postage and packing free within the UK).